ANIMAL
Tricks and Treks

AMAZING
ANIMAL JOURNEYS
by William Caper

Animal Class
by Susan Schott Karr

GLOBE FEARON

Pearson Learning Group

CONTENTS

AMAZING ANIMAL JOURNEYS

Animal Class

AMAZING ANIMAL JOURNEYS

by William Caper

CHAPTER 1

Nature's Round-Trip Ticket

What's the longest trip you have ever been on? Across your state? Across the country? Across an ocean? Did you know there are animals that go from one side of Earth to the other every year? It's true. Animals go on journeys that are hard to believe. Some birds fly higher than airplanes. Some fish swim from tiny streams all the way to the ocean, and later, swim back to the same streams. Scientists don't even know how they do it! These animal journeys are enormous tests of endurance. Some are truly **astounding**.

For example, a bird called the arctic tern actually flies as many miles as it takes to fly around the world. Another amazing animal, the elephant seal, swims thousands of miles each year. Where does it end up? It ends up on the same beach it started from.

These long trips are called **migrations**. A **migration** is when a group of animals travels from one area, or **ecosystem**, to another. These trips can take months.

Some animals travel when it's time to have their babies. Others leave to find **nourishment** when food becomes scarce where they are. A **migration** is like a round-trip ticket for an animal. However, animals don't fly in planes, ride in trains, or drive cars. They don't have maps that show them where to go, either.

All of these animals go on amazing journeys. Can you identify each one?

So how do **migrating** animals find their way to places thousands of miles from where they start? Some use special senses. People have five senses: sight, hearing, taste, smell, and touch. Most animals have the same senses as people. In many animals, these senses are better developed. For example, some birds find their way by using landmarks such as rivers and mountains. These birds have **astounding** eyesight. They can see and follow landmarks as they fly high above them. Some animals have senses that people don't have. Has anyone ever told you that you have a good sense of direction? Well, some birds have a *real* sense of direction! This special sense works like a compass inside the birds' brains. It gives them the ability to navigate by sensing in which direction to fly. Other birds find their way by sensing the position of the sun during the day and the stars at night. Birds aren't the only animals that find their way using the sun and stars. Some beetles use the sun to determine in which direction to fly, too. Some fish use the sun to help them find their way in the ocean.

Different animals use different methods to navigate more than thousands of miles. You are about to read about five wild animals and their incredible **migrations**. Get ready to soar through the air, glide beneath the ocean, and thunder across the land on some truly amazing animal journeys.

CHAPTER 2

Endless Summer

When the weather turns cold, people pretty much just have to deal with it. We put on our winter coats, dig out our winter hats from the back of our closets, and wait for the winter to go away. Birds, however, handle the cold a little differently.

Lots of birds head for warmer places. Geese and ducks fly south when their home **ecosystems** start getting chilly. It **tends** to be warmer in the South than it is in the North, so the odds of freezing to death are greatly reduced! Even more important, it is easier for birds to find food where it is warm. It's hard to find a seed below 2 feet of snow or catch a fish when a pond is frozen.

So geese and ducks stay in the South for several months, then fly back to the North when spring comes again. Most **migrate** anywhere from a few hundred to a few thousand miles round trip. That's a long way, but it doesn't even come close to the distance an arctic tern travels.

What is an arctic tern? An arctic tern is a cousin to the sea gull, only it's a lot smaller. It weighs less than 2 pounds and has a **relatively** short wingspan—about 31 inches from the tip of one wing to the other. Some sea gulls have a wingspan twice as long as that.

So how far does this little bird **migrate**? It travels more than 22,000 miles *every year*. That's almost the same as the distance around our planet! The arctic tern **basically** flies around the world every year. The life span of an arctic tern is about 20 years. So, during its lifetime, this bird covers more than 440,000 miles. That's nearly the same distance as flying to the Moon and back to Earth again!

Before we follow the terns on their **migration**, let's find out more about this little bird. Arctic terns live on the coasts of continents and islands of the Atlantic, Pacific, and Arctic oceans and the Bering Sea. These areas are all in the Arctic region, near Earth's North Pole.

Terns mate and hatch their eggs in these places. How a male tern attracts a female is also kind of unusual. First, the male catches a fish. Then, he flies very low, carrying the fish over the female. This low pass is called a fish flight. If she's attracted to him and his fish, she follows him, and they mate. The female tern then lays her eggs in tall grass or on a rock. Why? The Arctic has no trees! **Deprived** of trees, the terns have to make do with what they have. To protect the eggs, they divebomb any predators that go too near.

When the eggs hatch, the parents feed small fish to their chicks. The parents feed the young terns until they can fly. By the time terns can fly, it's time for them to go on their first **migration**.

These arctic tern parents are feeding their hatchlings.

Arctic Terns Really Hate Winter!

Arctic terns journey from **basically** as far north as you can get on Earth to about as far south. That means they go from the Arctic near the North Pole to Antarctica near the South Pole. Why? When it's winter in the Arctic, it's summer in the Antarctic. Going south gives the arctic tern two summers—and no winters! When the terns get to Antarctica, there are long hours of daylight and **ample** food. These conditions are just what the birds need.

Arctic terns start flying south in August. Arctic terns from all over the northern breeding ranges join with one another for the trip. The terns that start from islands near Canada, in the North Atlantic Ocean, fly to the southern tip of Greenland. There, they join terns that have been nesting on the Greenland coast. Together, they cross the Atlantic Ocean and join terns coming from Iceland and the northeastern coast of North America. The terns then fly south together, along the west coast of Africa.

Near the African coast, the birds split into two groups. One group continues south along the coast of Africa until it arrives in Antarctica. Smaller groups may split off in an eastward direction toward Antarctica. The other group turns west and crosses the Atlantic Ocean again, going toward Brazil. Then, the group splits into two again. Some birds follow the South American coast to Antarctica. Others stay farther out to sea on their flight south.

Meanwhile, arctic terns that live in Alaska are also flying toward Antarctica. These birds fly along the western coasts of North and South America. Eventually, they join the arctic terns that fly south along the east coast of South America.

All of the terns stay in Antarctica for several months. Then, as winter approaches, they fly all the way back to their breeding grounds in the north.

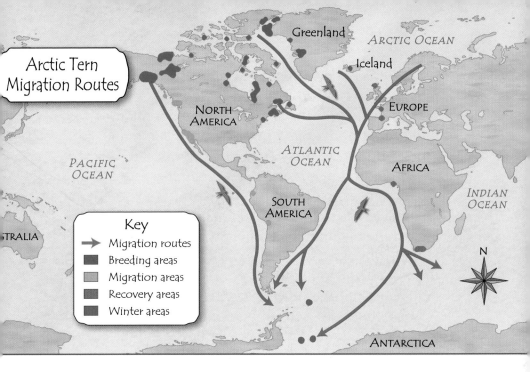

Arctic Tern Migration Routes

North America · Greenland · ARCTIC OCEAN · Iceland · EUROPE · PACIFIC OCEAN · ATLANTIC OCEAN · AFRICA · INDIAN OCEAN · SOUTH AMERICA · AUSTRALIA · ANTARCTICA · N

Key
→ Migration routes
■ Breeding areas
■ Migration areas
■ Recovery areas
■ Winter areas

Arctic terns are amazing for reasons other than the distance of their **migration**. For example, during their journey arctic terns almost never land, even though they have **ample** opportunity to do so. They don't even stop to eat. When they hunt fish, they swoop down out of the sky, catch a fish near the water's surface, and keep going. They even sleep in the air. How? Only one-half of their brain sleeps at a time! This little bird's ability to stay in the air for so long makes it truly incredible.

Arctic terns have webbed feet like ducks and geese, so you would think they would be good swimmers, too, right? Why don't they just land on the water and paddle for a few miles to rest their wings? The answer is that their feet are very small, so they can't swim very well.

Here's another cool fact about the arctic tern. Days are very long in both the Arctic and Antarctic summers. During each summer, the sun doesn't set at all. Because the arctic tern spends summers in both regions, it sees more daylight in 1 year than any other animal on the planet.

Now you know when, why, and how far arctic terns **migrate**. So how do they find their way? Scientists are still searching for the answer to this question. We said earlier that some birds use the stars like maps. Do arctic terns? The answer is—maybe not.

To get from the Arctic to the Antarctic, terns have to cross from the northern half of Earth to the southern half. The halves of Earth are called hemispheres. The night sky in each hemisphere has different stars in it. If the stars in the night sky change with each hemisphere, how could the terns know where they are when they fly from one hemisphere to the other? Scientists still aren't sure.

Scientists are sure of one thing, though. They know that there is one arctic tern that flew even farther than most. This tern flew an **astounding** 15,500 miles! Here's how scientists know that. The arctic tern was tagged in northern Sweden, in June 2003. Tagging a bird means putting a small metal ring on its leg. The ring identifies the bird. It also tells where and when the bird was tagged.

This bird was then found in December 2003, on Stewart Island in New Zealand. If measured in a straight line, the bird flew about 11,000 miles. That is **basically** a normal number of miles. However, the scientists were tracking this bird by its tag throughout its entire journey, and the bird did not fly in a straight line. First, it flew south, along Africa's west coast. When it reached South Africa, it turned east and began to fly toward New Zealand. By the time it landed, it had flown 15,500 miles one way. Now that's **endurance**! As you now know, the arctic tern is the only bird in the world that could make that amazing journey.

CHAPTER 3

Elephants of the Sea

While some arctic terns are flying high above the Pacific Ocean from the Arctic to the Antarctic, there is another animal making a dangerous journey in the ocean below. Sometimes it has to dive thousands of feet to avoid being eaten by a killer whale. It also has to eat as many fish and squid as it possibly can, because when it's on land, it can't eat a thing. This animal is a mammal, just like you. Except this mammal has flippers instead of legs, and it can hold its breath for hours.

What is this strange creature? We are talking about the enormous elephant seal. Elephant seals are mammals that have **adapted** so that they can live on land *and* in the water. Elephant seals belong to a group of mammals called pinnipeds. There are three main kinds of pinnipeds: the walrus, the eared seal, and the earless seal. The elephant seal is an earless seal. It is the second-largest sea mammal on Earth, after the whale.

Elephant seals can dive thousands of feet underwater. Some elephant seals can dive more than 5,000 feet. That's the same as 16 football fields. Seals often stay underwater for more than 20 minutes on a single dive. The longest known dive for an elephant seal is 119 minutes, or almost 2 hours underwater. That's like holding your breath for the length of an entire movie.

There are two kinds of elephant seals—northern and southern. Southern elephant seals **inhabit** the Atlantic and Indian oceans near Antarctica. They stay in those waters their whole lives. Northern elephant seals live near the west coast of North America, from Mexico to Canada. Some of these elephant seals are **migrating** more than 11,300 miles every year! That's the longest **migration** of any mammal.

A lot of what we know about how elephant seals move comes from a group of seals that **inhabit** a rookery near the coast of California. A rookery is where seals go to mate and to molt. (Molting is when a seal sheds all of its skin. Yikes!) This rookery is at Año Nuevo State Reserve in northern California. Scientists went there to put tracking devices on 47 elephant seals.

These tracking devices allowed scientists to follow the seals wherever they went. How? The devices sent out signals—a different one for each elephant seal. A satellite in space then mapped where the signals were coming from in the ocean. Scientists could follow each seal by following its special signal.

Scientists already knew that both male and female seals leave the Año Nuevo rookery after breeding in March. The females return first to molt in May and then head back out to sea for 8 months. The males return to molt in midsummer and then embark on a 4-month ocean trip.

With the tracking devices, scientists learned that the males travel directly to one feeding area and stay there until they are done feeding. Only then do they head back to the rookery.

Female elephant seals have a different **migration** pattern. This was a big surprise to the scientists. Scientists thought males and females fed on the same sea animals, in the same places, at the same time, but they were wrong! The females travel all over the northeastern Pacific Ocean. They also eat everywhere they swim—not just in one feeding area like the males.

Scientists were also surprised to find that males use the same route every time they **migrate**, but females do not. Females keep taking different routes. Scientists thought the different habits of the females were really weird. Think about it. Wouldn't it be strange if you took a different road to school every day?

They also found out that male and female elephant seals dive differently. Males dive to the bottom of the ocean. They then feed on the animals that live on the ocean floor, like skates, rays, and small sharks. The females' dives are all over the place! It looks as if they are chasing prey that moves up and down in the water, like squids.

Scientists thought the difference in size between males and females might have something to do with the way they eat. The males can weigh almost 6,000 pounds, or as much as a truck. It's kind of hard to chase little squids when you are that big. Females weigh closer to a thousand pounds, or the size of a big motorcycle. That means they have a better chance of **adapting** their dives to catch fast-moving sea animals such as squids. Male elephant seals also gain **substantially** more weight during their travels than the females do, despite spending less time at sea feeding. Males probably find more food, eat higher-quality food, or both.

The male's trunklike snout and the large size of this mammal give the elephant seal its name.

13

Size Counts

It turns out that putting on weight is very important to male elephant seals. Why? The male's size helps him win fights with other males. By hunting for more and more food, however, the males take big risks. Males stay closer to shore than females do. There is more food there. Unfortunately, killer whales and great white sharks like to hunt for food in the same places! Male elephant seals are big, but they are still no match for a killer whale or a great white shark. Females who look for food in the open ocean are **relatively** less likely to encounter these deadly predators.

For the males that survive, putting on all of that extra weight is worth it. When they get back to the rookery, they have a better chance of winning a harem of females and keeping it. Females arrive back at the rookery first and form groups called harems. Harems can have up to 50 females. When the males arrive, they each claim a harem of females. Only one male, also called an alpha bull, lives with each harem. He will mate with every female in his harem.

Other bulls that want access to his harem challenge the alpha bull almost daily. These bulls challenge the alpha male by trumpeting through their trunks. The alpha trumpets back, warning the other bulls to stay away.

If a bull does not back off, the two bulls fight. During the battle, the bulls smash into each other. These fights can be bloody. Most older alpha bulls have tough scar tissue on their necks and chests. This scar tissue is from fights the alpha bulls have had. It helps protect them from getting seriously hurt in future fights.

The bulls fight until one wins. If the alpha bull wins, he keeps his harem. The weaker male then keeps a **relatively** safe distance from the harem and the alpha bull.

While they are at the rookery, male and female elephant seals don't eat. They only eat while they are at sea. Nursing females can lose 300 to 500 pounds while they are on land. Their pups, however, **thrive**. The female's milk is very rich in fat, so pups get the **nourishment** they need.

After the pups are a few weeks old, the females mate with the alpha bull again. Then, they return to the ocean. By now they are extremely hungry. They have been **depriving** themselves of food since they came onto land. After the females leave, the males return to the ocean, too.

The pups remain behind. They live off fat stored in their bodies. They lie close to one another to stay warm. After several weeks, the pups have to swim to find food on their own. Then, they, too, leave the rookery and swim north, beginning their first **migration**.

In spring and summer, young seals and older seals return to rookeries to molt. Elephant seals molt their outer skin and fur very fast. After they molt, the seals return to the ocean, covered with a new coat of silver fur. Now, they begin their second **migration** north. They will stay in the water until they haul out again, months later, to mate at the same rookery.

A mother seal barks at her young pup.

There used to be millions of elephant seals. Then, almost all of them disappeared. Why? People killed them.

Elephant seals have thick layers of fat called blubber. This blubber gives them **ample** protection from cold water. During the 1800s, people hunted elephant seals for their blubber. People turned the blubber into oil. They used the oil to make soap, paint, and fuel for lamps. They also used it to waterproof their clothes.

So many elephant seals were killed that by the late 1800s they were in danger of becoming extinct. In the early 1900s, governments started passing laws protecting elephant seals. The United States has passed two laws to protect elephant seals in U.S. waters. The Marine Mammal Protection Act makes it illegal to hunt elephant seals and other sea animals in these waters. Another law says that people must stay at least 20 feet away from elephant seals at all times.

These laws have helped elephant seal populations **thrive**. Elephant seals are no longer facing extinction. Their population was down to almost nothing 100 years ago. Today, the elephant seal population is about 150,000, and it is growing.

Although northern elephant seals are protected, people can visit some rookeries. You can even visit Año Nuevo, the rookery you read about earlier where scientists tagged and studied the seals. People who go there can take guided tours to learn about elephant seals. At a rookery named Piedras Blancas, north of Cambria, California, volunteers give talks and answer people's questions about elephant seals.

At these rookeries, people can watch bulls challenge each other for control of a harem. They might see young pups that have just been born and hear them call to their mothers. These are the pups that will soon be on their own, following their mothers' and fathers' paths in one of the animal world's most amazing **migrations**.

CHAPTER 4

Against the Current

Did you know that two-thirds of Earth is covered in water? There is fresh water in streams and lakes, and there is salt water in the seas and oceans. Most fish live their lives in either fresh water or salt water. A salmon can live in both! How a salmon gets from a stream to an ocean and back again is probably the coolest story about **endurance** you will ever hear.

Salmon start off in freshwater streams and lakes, where they hatch out of eggs. Sooner or later, they have an urge to swim all the way to an ocean. They swim around in the ocean eating, getting bigger and bigger, until it's time to breed. Where do you think they go to breed? They swim from the ocean all the way back to their home streams. Sometimes this means swimming thousands of miles. The salmon actually swim all the way upstream to the place where they were born. Their journey is very long and difficult.

Going upstream, they swim against **substantial** currents. Yet the salmon keep going, refusing to let anything hold them back. Any animal with the **endurance** and perseverance to swim against a rushing river is worth getting to know a little better.

There are eight species of salmon. Amago are the smallest kind. They're about 5 to 9 inches long. Chinook are the largest. They can be as long as 3 feet and usually weigh about 22 pounds. Some of them grow up to 80 pounds! Can you imagine seeing an 80-pound fish swimming in a river? That's a big fish! Before we get to their swimming though, let's start at the very beginning, when the salmon are still in their eggs.

A salmon begins its life in fresh water. Most salmon breed in fresh water in the summer or fall. Breeding is also called spawning, and how salmon spawn is also very interesting.

Female salmon lay their eggs in gravel at the bottom of streams or in the shallow water of lakes. First, a female turns on her side and swishes her tail around to create a nest in the gravel. The female and male go into the nest together and swim in place very fast, side by side. It kind of looks like they're dancing. The female releases her eggs, and the male fertilizes them. Then, the female swims a short distance, creates another nest, and the male follows. The gravel dug from each nest protects the eggs that were just laid.

A spawning female lays from 2,000 to 17,000 eggs. It takes from 2 to 7 months for them to hatch. The newborn salmon are called fry. The fry hide in the gravel nests for several weeks. They get **nourishment** from the yolk in their egg sac. When the yolk is gone, the fry leave their nests to find food.

Why do salmon lay their eggs in rocky nests?

Some species of salmon then stay in fresh water for a long time. One kind of Atlantic salmon stays in fresh water for 5 years! Other kinds of salmon start swimming to the ocean right after they wriggle out of the gravel. For them, the urge to migrate is unstoppable.

When a salmon is ready to **migrate**, it races down its river to the ocean as fast as it can. Going downstream makes swimming easier for the salmon. Yet there are many dangers along the way, and most of the salmon never reach the ocean. The fish face **substantial** challenges, including birds, bears and other wild animals, and barriers created by people. High dams stop many salmon. Others get stuck in reservoirs that people have built or die when they swim through polluted water.

The salmon that survive the trip are pretty lucky. Only a handful of salmon from each nest make it all the way to the ocean. Once they get there, those lucky few have to adjust from fresh water to salt water right away. If they don't, they can actually dry out while swimming in the salty ocean! To survive in the ocean, their bodies have to **adapt** to the salt water. Chemical changes in the salmon's body, and special cells in its gills, make this possible.

Salmon then live in salt water from 6 months to several years, depending on the species. While in the ocean, they eat squid, shrimp, and small fish. At sea, some salmon, such as the masu, live in a **relatively** small area. Others travel thousands of miles. Young sockeye, chum, and pink salmon in the North Pacific Ocean travel those thousands of miles. How do they do this? They swim with the powerful ocean currents. They not only travel very far out to sea, but they also move along at speeds up to ten times faster than they would be able to swim on their own.

Time to Go Home

No matter how far out to sea they swim, when it is time to spawn, salmon must return to the stream or lake in which they were born. How do they find their way back home? Scientists think that salmon have a few different ways of navigating their way through an ocean.

One way salmon do it is to follow the hills and valleys on the seafloor. The seafloor has ups and downs, just like dry land. Scientists think salmon may remember what the seafloor looks like. By sensing what is beneath them when they are swimming, salmon can figure out where they are.

There is **evidence** that salmon find their home stream by using their sense of smell. Scientists think they remember the scent of their home stream, and they follow this scent. Salmon are also great at sensing water temperature. This sense helps them find the stream they are looking for. They can remember the exact temperature of their home stream. They remember a temperature like people remember a street address!

When salmon finally make it back to fresh water, their bodies have to adjust again. Salmon stop eating. As they swim upstream, they use the fat stored in their body for **nourishment**. They also change color. In the ocean, salmon are mostly silver. As they travel upstream, chum salmon get purple streaks on their sides. Sockeye salmon turn bright red. Atlantic salmon become green or brown. In addition to changing color, salmon change shape on their way upriver. As male salmon swim upstream, their jaws change shape. Male pink salmon also grow a hump on their back.

The journey upriver can take several months. Some spawning grounds are close to the ocean. Some are far from it. Some chum salmon swim more than 2,000 miles to reach their spawning ground.

A dangerous surprise awaits these jumping salmon.

The return **migration** is harder than the journey to the ocean was. Bears and other animals prey on salmon. Still, most of the dangers come from people. For example, people on fishing boats wait for the returning salmon along the oceans' coasts. They drop nets into the water and catch millions of salmon each year.

When salmon reach fresh water, they face even more people who fish for them in rivers, streams, and lakes. In addition to swimming against a river current, salmon must fight dangerous rapids and leap over waterfalls. Luckily, salmon are superb jumpers. They can jump as high as 10 feet. Unfortunately, jumping 10 feet is not going to help a salmon if there's a 100-foot dam straight ahead!

Dams may be the biggest obstacle migrating salmon face. Many dams are too high for the fish to jump over. Some dams also have machinery that controls the height of the water on the other side. For bigger, older salmon, the machinery is a real **menace**. It kills thousands of them every year. Young salmon can sometimes survive swimming through the machinery. What can a big, old salmon do when faced with a 100-foot dam and a lot of dangerous dam machinery? It can swim through a pass.

To help **migrating** salmon, people have built fish passes. These passes allow fish to go around or over a dam. One kind of fish pass is the fish ladder. Fish ladders are a series of steps built next to a dam. The steps have water running over them. By jumping from step to step, salmon slowly climb over the dam.

Another kind of fish pass is the fish lock. Fish swim into a compartment called a lock at the bottom of a dam. Gates close, and more water flows into the lock. The height of the water increases until the fish are raised to the height of the dam. Then, the lock gates open and the fish swim on their way. Fish passes help thousands of salmon **migrate** each year. So people aren't always bad news when it comes to salmon!

Once salmon make it back to their home stream, they spawn. The salmon lay and fertilize their eggs in the same place that they started as eggs years ago. The next part of a salmon's life is the saddest. After completing their incredible journey, most types of salmon die after they spawn. Their bodies age rapidly in a way that is similar to how other animals age over their lifetime. The thing is, for salmon, it all happens in a couple of weeks, and the salmon die.

However, there are some Atlantic salmon that don't die after they spawn. When their eggs are laid and fertilized, these salmon head right back to the ocean. There, they go through the whole cycle again. They feed in the ocean until they have enough **nourishment** to make it back to fresh water to spawn again. Some Atlantic salmon actually make the incredible journey three times in their lives. A fish that makes the round trip once is probably the strongest animal you will ever read about. A fish that can **migrate** *three* times is definitely one of the strongest animals in the world.

CHAPTER 5

Coldblooded Courage

By now, it should be **evident** to you that elephant seals, arctic terns, and salmon are tough animals. Now we're going to tell you about another species that is just as tough. What do you think it will be? A gorilla? A lion? A wolf? No—how about a little butterfly?

Every year, as winter approaches, millions of monarch butterflies leave the northern United States and Canada and fly thousands of miles south. Why? Monarchs can't stand cold weather. In fact, just one freezing day could kill them! Butterflies—like all insects—are coldblooded. That means a monarch's body temperature **basically** matches the temperature of the air around it.

Mammals and birds are warmblooded. Their body temperature stays about the same regardless of how hot or cold the temperature is. Because monarchs are coldblooded, they cannot survive in the cold at all. So, they have to **migrate** to warmer places. Their timing has to be perfect, too. If they wait 1 day too long, the weather might suddenly become very cold. If that happens, their bodies will be **deprived** of the warmth they need, and they will freeze to death.

We said monarchs were as tough as elephant seals. They don't sound very tough so far! How can an animal or insect be tough if one cold night will kill it?

That's a good question. Monarchs really are tough because of their amazing **migration**. Some monarchs fly more than 2,000 miles. That is a **substantial** distance for a tiny insect. During their journey, monarchs can fly as many as 80 miles in a day. Can you imagine walking or running 80 miles a day? Now you're starting to understand how tough these butterflies are.

North American monarchs start their **migration** in August. They reach their homes on the California coast and in Mexico in October. When monarch butterflies get to their warm-weather destinations, they gather together on tree trunks and branches. These butterfly gatherings are called clusters.

After all you have read about **migrations**, it may not surprise you to learn that monarchs return to the same area each year. What may **astound** you is that monarchs return to the exact same tree! Once they cluster on their favorite tree, the butterflies hibernate for the winter.

In the spring, monarchs wake up, mate, and then make the return trip, **migrating** north. Not all the monarchs that flew south return all the way north, however. As they fly north, female monarchs stop and lay eggs. Then, these females die. After the new generation of butterflies hatches and matures, it continues north.

As with most **migrating** animals, monarchs face danger and life-threatening challenges along their trip. How do these insects survive such a long journey? How do they survive the winter while they hibernate?

Hibernating monarch butterflies completely cover the trunk of this tree.

As the monarchs fly south, they sip nectar from flowers to build up fat. This fat is stored in their abdomens. Monarchs sip so much nectar while flying south, they actually gain weight. They then live off the stored fat while they hibernate. In addition, they need the stored fat when they fly north the following spring, too. Why? Like salmon, monarchs **deprive** themselves of food on their return trip.

Monarchs do something else similar to salmon. Remember when we talked about salmon catching rides on ocean currents? Some scientists think that monarch butterflies catch rides on air currents when they fly south. These strong winds help the monarchs fly long distances faster and with less effort.

What about predators? Monarch butterflies have one great defense against **menacing** birds and animals. They're poisonous! Monarchs are poisonous because they eat poisonous milkweed plants. If a predator bites a monarch, it tastes the nasty milkweed poison and usually lets the monarch go. If a predator accidentally eats a monarch, it gets really sick, and it will never eat another monarch again! Adult monarchs also have hard bodies and hard, large wings, which help them to survive a predator's bite.

Most predators know better than to bite a monarch in the first place. The monarch's bright colors make it **evident** that it is poisonous. Why? Lots of insects that do not taste good use bright colors to warn predators. After eating one or two bad-tasting, brightly colored insects, most predators avoid them from then on.

As you can tell, we know a lot about monarch butterflies and their amazing journey. However, there is still a lot people don't know. How do monarchs find the same winter sites year after year? How do young monarchs find their way north after their birth? How do monarchs find the very same tree? No one knows.

Braving the Cold

Deer can be found all over the United States. Somehow, they have been able to live right alongside people without too much of a problem. Most deer in the United States are either mule deer or white-tailed deer. These deer weigh about 150 to 300 pounds. That sounds like a lot, right? It is nothing compared to a caribou.

Caribou are *big* deer. Male caribou can weigh as much as 660 pounds and grow to 5 feet tall at the shoulder. Mule deer and white-tailed deer **tend** to top out around 4 feet. Caribou **inhabit** the forests, mountains, and plains of Canada and Alaska. They're also found in parts of Greenland and the state of Washington.

Caribou have **adapted** well to their habitats. In their cold northern **ecosystems**, freezing temperatures and powerful storms blanket the land with thick ice and snow. Caribou have very wide hooves that help them walk on snow. They also have two layers of fur. The underlayer is soft and fluffy. The top layer is a thick coat of hair. Each hair on a caribou's hide is hollow. Inside the hollow hair is air. The air keeps the caribou's body heat from escaping.

There's another part of caribou that changes during the year—their hooves. Just as dogs and cats have pads on their paws, caribou have pads on their hooves. However, the caribou's hooves keep changing. In summer, when the ground is softer, the pads are soft to help the caribou walk on soggy ground. In winter, the pads **tend** to get harder to help the caribou walk on ice. In addition, during winter, stiff hairs grow between the caribou's pads. These hairs help keep caribou from slipping on ice.

In many species of deer, only the males grow antlers. Male caribou, called bulls, and female caribou, called cows, both have antlers. The antlers of the male caribou can grow to 5 feet from end to end. The antlers of female caribou can grow to 20 inches from end to end.

Both males and females shed their antlers each year and grow a new set. Males lose their antlers at the end of mating season, in October. Females lose their antlers when they give birth, in early spring.

Caribou eat grass, mushrooms, and entire young trees. In winter, their main food is lichen. Lichen is a kind of plant that grows on rocks. Caribou use their hooves to scrape snow off the rocks so they can access the lichen.

Caribou live in herds. Like female elephant seals, the female caribou form groups called harems. Like male elephant seals, caribou bulls battle each other for the harems during the mating season.

Bulls chase one another. They duel, using their antlers as weapons. These battles can be violent and serious. Sometimes the bulls become exhausted or injured. Then, they become easy targets for predators such as wolves and grizzly bears.

Caribou live in some of the most challenging habitats in North America. Part of the caribou's range is above the tree line. The tree line is the point above which trees do not grow. Why don't they grow there? The land is too high. The winds this high are so strong that they would knock over a young tree. Up high, the temperature also is very cold for very long periods. These regions have one of the harshest climates in the world. In these places, it becomes hard to find food. That's why caribou **migrate**.

These caribou bulls face off for battle.

Each year, caribou travel as much as 800 miles between the southern and northern parts of their range. That is not nearly as far as some of the other **migrations** in this book. However, the landscape of the caribou's **ecosystem** makes the trip just as difficult.

Caribou head south in the fall and early winter, traveling across tundra in huge herds. Tundra is a treeless plain found mainly in cold northern regions.

A caribou herd can include thousands of animals. **Migrating** caribou move along an exact path. They may go extremely fast. They might keep moving day and night, without stopping to rest or eat. The sight of a caribou herd can be **astounding**. People who have seen thousands of caribou moving together have described it as being "like a river across the landscape."

Caribou stay in the southern part of their range until early spring. It is still very cold, even in the southern part of their range, but the caribou can **thrive**. Why? One reason is the bulls have stopped fighting. Another reason is, because the caribou are farther south, the snow is often softer. This soft snow makes it easier for the caribou to find lichen, so they are not **deprived** of food.

Caribou Calves

In early spring, caribou head back to the northern part of their range. Like the journey south, the northward **migration** is very dangerous. Deep snow can slow the herd. Melting ice may cause rivers to flood. Caribou are strong swimmers. This is another way they have **adapted** to their habitat.

In the northern part of their range, caribou have their calving grounds—the area where females give birth to their young. A young caribou is called a calf.

Most calves are born in June. At this time of year, the calving grounds have **ample** vegetation which provides plenty of food for the caribou. The nursing mothers are able to find **nourishment** and feed their young.

The best calving grounds are areas where there are few predators. However, even in the safest calving grounds, caribou must always keep a watchful eye out for grizzly bears, wolves, and eagles that might **menace** their young. Calves also face danger from fierce storms. Luckily for their parents, young caribou are well-suited to their habitat. A calf that is only a few days old can already run faster than a person!

In the middle of summer, caribou herds break into smaller groups. These groups wander to different areas of the range to find food. They also move to windy, open spaces to try to escape insects. Even though the caribou's habitat is very cold, in summer the air is thick with flies and mosquitoes. These insects constantly bite the caribou. Flies even lay eggs in the caribou's fur. As many as 2,000 flies have been found on one caribou!

The caribou's natural enemies include wolves, lynx, wolverines, and grizzly bears. Yet the biggest threat may come from people. Caribou are an important source of food for people who live in these northern regions. Caribou are also valued for their antlers and hides.

Caribou also face problems because of other human activity in their habitat. They live in areas where there may be large deposits of oil and gas. As people search for these resources, they change the land where caribou live and **migrate**. People build roads. They bring in heavy equipment. When gas or oil is found, drilling stations and pipelines are built.

These activities destroy vegetation. They might result in there being fewer areas where caribou can safely have their young. They can make calving grounds less accessible to the caribou. There is also the danger of oil or chemical spills destroying these areas.

One type of caribou, the woodland caribou, has suffered a great deal from human activity. The woodland caribou is now listed as an endangered species. It is in danger of becoming extinct in all, or in a large part, of its range.

Woodland caribou live in the northwestern United States and northern Canada. Their habitat has been so greatly affected by human activity that in some places they are now limited to staying in the northern parts of their range.

Caribou face yet another threat. In some places there are more white-tailed deer in the woodland caribou's habitat. The deer present a special problem for the caribou. White-tailed deer carry a tiny worm that does not affect the deer. However, this worm can kill caribou. If caribou catch the worm from contact with the deer, they usually die.

As people search for resources, it is important to take the needs of animals into account. If they don't, there is the risk that some day there may be no herds of **migrating** caribou, and other animals like them, flowing "like a river across the landscape."

A caribou herd sticks close together as it migrates.

Migration and Us

Whether they take place on land, in the air, or under water, animal **migrations** fascinate us. Scientists have studied **migrations** closely. They know how mature arctic terns navigate as they cross the world. Scientists can tell us how salmon in an open ocean find the streams and lakes where they were born.

Yet we still don't know what powerful force drives salmon back to their home waters. We don't quite understand how monarch butterflies are able to fly thousands of miles to the same trees every year. We wonder how young arctic terns recognize a night sky they have never seen.

Migrations can help us learn about our world. People who visit elephant seal rookeries gain a better understanding of these incredible creatures and the oceans they live in. Learning about the caribou can encourage people to think about how our need for resources affects these animals.

We are slowly solving many of nature's puzzles. Yet we may never learn all there is to know about animal **migration**. That's why these amazing animal journeys have been called one of nature's best-kept secrets.

Animal Class

by Susan Schott Karr

Chapter 1

ANIMAL TEACHERS

A man has a heart attack while driving his car. He slumps over, unconscious. His dog, Sparky, is riding beside him. Sparky jumps over and puts his paws on the car's steering wheel. He barks out of the window at a police car. The police car follows.

To stop the car, Sparky jumps down and takes his owner's foot in his mouth. He moves it off the gas pedal. The car slows. Sparky pushes on the brake pedal with his paws. The car screeches to a stop! Sparky jumps out the window and barks.

"You're a hero!" the police officer says.

"Cut!" someone yells. "Great job, Sparky!"

What just happened? A crew was taping a scene for a TV show! Everyone in this scene was an actor, including Sparky. He wasn't really driving the car—a person was driving it by remote control.

However, Sparky had to learn to put his paws on a steering wheel. He also had to learn how to bark at the right time, pull a person's foot off a gas pedal, and push on a brake pedal. How did he learn to do these things? Someone trained him.

People all around the world train animals to do all kinds of things. Camels and elephants have been trained to take people from place to place. Donkeys, horses, and water buffalo have been taught to haul heavy loads. Pigeons have even been trained to take messages from one place to another.

It takes practice, patience, and experience to get an animal to do something that isn't a natural action for it to do. So what makes a good animal trainer? First, a good trainer has to be able to **interpret** an animal's behavior. The trainer needs to **comprehend** what a dog means when it is barking, or what a camel means when it sits down and refuses to move.

A trainer must also be good at communicating with an animal. Trainers have to **convey** to the animal that it should obey voice, hand, and other commands. Trainers also have to be **effective** at dealing with both animals and people. For instance, a person who trains guide dogs to work with people must also teach a blind person to work with the dog.

Maybe the most important part of being a good trainer is liking animals. If you are an animal trainer, you are around animals all of the time, **participating** in their care. If you are going to be **exposed** to animals every day, being friends with them makes life a lot more fun.

Most animal trainers in the United States work in zoos, circuses, dog kennels, horse stables, marine theme parks, or guide-dog schools. Some also work in people's homes and on movie sets. There are about 14,600 animal trainers in the United States. Who knows—maybe someday you'll want to be one, too.

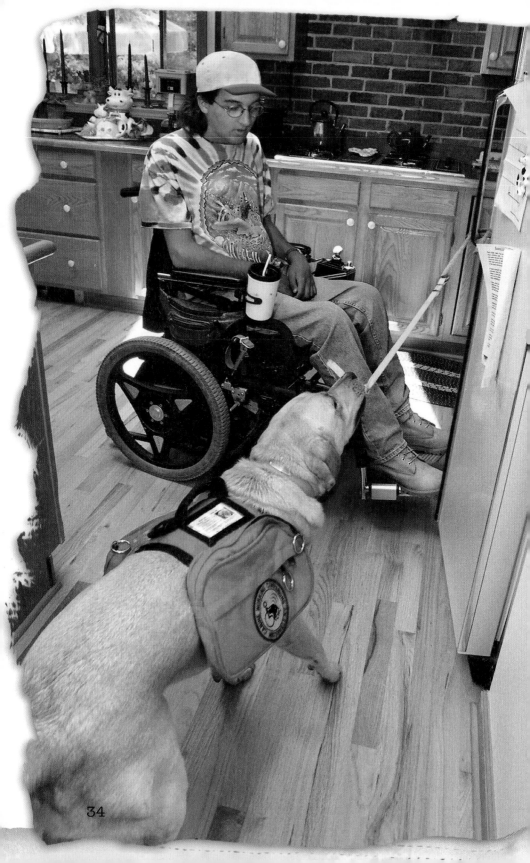

Chapter 2

DOGS TO THE RESCUE

Dogs were the first animals ever to live with humans. That's probably why they are called "man's best friend." Over the years, dogs have helped people hunt, haul, and be happy! Today, dogs are an important part of millions of people's lives.

Most dogs are just pets. However, many are trained as service dogs. This means the dogs learn how to do a service for a person. For example, some service dogs visit sick kids in the hospital. Having a visit from a friendly dog can make a kid who is ill feel much better. Other dogs visit people in nursing homes or prisons. Some prison inmates even **participate** in programs in which they train dogs to help other people.

Dogs are also trained to rescue people. For instance, there are dogs that save people caught in an avalanche! An avalanche is caused by a huge amount of snow breaking off a snowpack and crashing down a mountain with amazing speed and power. A rescue dog uses its sense of smell to search for people trapped under the snow. It barks when it smells someone. Then, rescue workers know where to dig out the victim.

There are even service dogs that help kids learn how to read. How? The dogs sit with students while the students read out loud. Of course, the dogs can't **comprehend** what a student is reading. It's just that sometimes, kids are more willing to read to dogs than to their classmates. Why? Dogs don't notice mistakes! Kids who read to dogs often end up feeling better about their reading skills.

◀ **A trained companion dog helps its owner by opening the refrigerator.**

Of course, before a dog can sit still for a book reading, sniff out a snow-covered person, or behave in a hospital, it has to learn a few things. Animal trainers are good at using **aspects** of a dog's personality in the dog's training. For example, dogs are pack animals. That means they naturally follow the leader of their pack. A good dog trainer knows how to act like a dog's "pack leader." Then, whatever the trainer says, goes!

However, being a leader doesn't mean **provoking** a dog or being bossy. Dogs love to play and have fun. Good trainers use this **aspect** of a dog's personality by making training more like playing.

Dogs also love to eat! Giving the dog a treat is a great example of positive **reinforcement**. So is a pat or a hug. Most trainers combine their pack-leader status, a fun environment, and some kind of **reinforcement** for good behavior to train their dogs.

Now that you have an idea about how dogs are trained, let's look at one of the most amazing things that dogs have been trained to do: seeing for blind people.

▲ **This rescue dog was trained to save people trapped in avalanches.**

"Seeing" for Blind People

Dogs have been trained to guide blind people since right after World War I. The first school was in Germany. The dogs trained there helped soldiers who had been blinded in the war. Dorothy Eustis, an American living in Switzerland, wrote about the school in a story that appeared in an American magazine. A blind man in the United States, Morris Frank, heard about the story. He wrote to her and asked her to have a dog trained for him. In return, he said he would start a guide-dog training school in the United States.

Morris Frank got his guide dog, a female German shepherd that he named "Buddy." He then founded his guide-dog school in 1929 in Nashville, Tennessee. He called it The Seeing Eye, Inc. Soon after, he moved the school to Morristown, New Jersey, where it is today.

There are many other guide-dog schools around the country, but The Seeing Eye is still the most famous. Since its start, The Seeing Eye school has matched 13,000 dogs with more than 6,000 blind people in the United States and Canada. The school trains dogs to help blind people and also teaches people how to train the dogs. Let's take a closer look at The Seeing Eye's **procedure** for training dogs *and* trainers.

First, The Seeing Eye school raises its dogs. German shepherds, golden retrievers, and Labrador retrievers are the best guide-dog breeds. They are gentle, intelligent, and a good, medium size.

Families who work with guide-dog schools adopt the puppies when they are about seven weeks old. The puppies live with these families full time. The families teach the puppies to obey certain commands, such as sit, no, stay, stop, down, and forward. The dogs stay with their foster families until they are about 18 months old. Then, they are ready to go back to the school for more intensive training.

The dogs then take part in a four-month course at The Seeing Eye. Each dog gets a sighted trainer. "We are all dog lovers," says one trainer. "We take great pride in knowing that the dogs under our care are healthy and happy."

Trainers review the commands the dogs have learned with their foster families. Then, they start adding new ones. First, the dogs have to **demonstrate** that they are comfortable walking beside the trainers. Next, the trainers teach the dogs to change direction on command.

One step in the training **procedure** is to get the dogs used to wearing a special harness. The harness helps the trainer—and later, the owner—hold onto the dog. Once a dog is used to its harness, it is trained to help its owner cross a street.

How does a dog learn to safely guide a blind person across a street? At The Seeing Eye school, trainers take the dogs to downtown Morristown. They start on quiet side streets. The dogs are trained to stop at a curb and then cross when the trainer can **indicate** that no cars are coming.

Once dogs are good at crossing a quiet street, they are taken to a busy street. They are trained to stop at the curb and then cross when the traffic stops at the light. The dogs also learn to avoid obstacles such as poles, signs, and people. They must learn to **indicate** to their blind owners that there are objects in the way. Guide dogs also learn "intelligent disobedience." They are trained to ignore a command if it would lead to dangerous consequences for their owner.

After four months, a Seeing Eye school dog is ready for its final exam. The dog is taken to downtown Morristown by a trainer who then puts on a blindfold. A second person comes along to watch and make sure the dog has learned everything it needs to know.

Once a dog passes its final exam, it is paired with a blind owner. A trainer works with the dog and its owner to teach them to work as a team. It takes about a month before the dog goes to live with its owner full time. All of the training is important, because some day, the dog may save its owner's life.

▲ A guide dog waits with its owner for the train doors to open.

Michael Hingson owes his life to his guide dog, Roselle. "Roselle helped save my life when we both escaped the World Trade Center tragedy," says Hingson. They were on the seventy-eighth floor of their building in the World Trade Center in New York City when a plane hit the building on September 11, 2001. Roselle, a yellow Lab, was asleep under Michael's desk.

The building began to fill with smoke, so Roselle led Michael to the stairs. They walked down 78 flights of steps. They were hot and tired. "Roselle was panting and wanted to drink the water that was pooled on the floor," said Michael, but they kept on going. Roselle led Michael to the home of a friend—and to safety. All of Roselle's training had definitely paid off.

Chapter 3

HORSE POWER

Have you ever ridden a horse? If you have, you know how scary and exciting it is to be in control of such a big, strong animal. If you haven't, try to imagine riding an animal that can weigh more than 1,000 pounds. It stands about five-and-a-half-feet tall at the shoulder. From the tip of its nose to the end of its tail, it is about nine feet long. Do you see how **aspects** of riding an animal this large can be dangerous? It takes a lot of patience and skill to ride a horse. It takes even more patience and skill to teach a horse to be ridden.

Any horse you ride probably will have already been trained before you ride it. Horses don't naturally like someone to get on top of them and tell them where to go. First, a horse has to be trained to understand that it can trust you to ride it. Then, it must be trained to **interpret** the commands you give it.

Horses are sensitive animals. Trainers have to be great communicators to **alter** a horse's behavior. To communicate **effectively**, a horse trainer has to get to know a horse the same way he or she would get to know a person. For example, some people hate to be told what to do, while some others don't mind it as much. The same is true for horses.

4000 BCE The first tamed horses are herded on the grassy lands of the Ukraine.

2000 BCE In ancient Greece, horses are trained for the Olympic Games, including horseback riding and chariot races.

600 CE In Europe, horses are used for warfare and farming.

| 5000 BCE | 4000 BCE | 3000 BCE | 2000 BCE | 1 CE | 200 CE | 400 CE | 600 CE |

▲ **A History of the Working Horse**

People have been training horses for different types of work for thousands of years. Through the years, horses have been trained for sport and to be ridden into battle by soldiers. They have pulled heavy loads—and, of course, they have been ridden from one place to another.

Trainers take advantage of horses' natural traits when teaching the animals to work. Horses are social animals. They live in herds and family groups. They are loyal and look after other horses in the herd. They defend their territory and take care of young horses.

To teach horses to be ridden, trainers try to be like members of the herd. The trainers are with the horses every day. That way, the horses are **exposed** to their trainers. Being part of the herd allows a trainer to help care for a new horse right after it is born.

A newborn horse is called a foal. One of the first things a trainer tries to **convey** is that the foal can trust the trainer. First, he or she talks gently to the foal, so the foal gets to know the trainer's voice. Then, the trainer strokes the foal with a soft brush and with his or her hands.

This **aspect** of the training is called gentling. The trainer is making sure the foal is calm and relaxed. One **indication** that the foal is making progress is whether or not it can relax when the trainer is near.

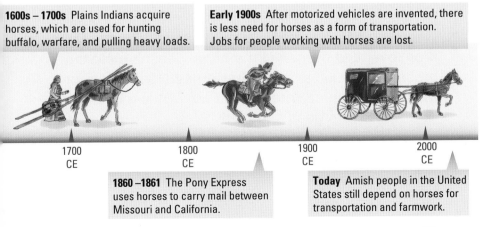

1600s – 1700s Plains Indians acquire horses, which are used for hunting buffalo, warfare, and pulling heavy loads.

Early 1900s After motorized vehicles are invented, there is less need for horses as a form of transportation. Jobs for people working with horses are lost.

1700 CE

1800 CE

1900 CE

2000 CE

1860 –1861 The Pony Express uses horses to carry mail between Missouri and California.

Today Amish people in the United States still depend on horses for transportation and farmwork.

Once a foal **demonstrates** that it's comfortable around the trainer, the trainer starts working with it. One of the first things the horse must learn is to wear a halter. A strap or a rope is tied to the halter and used to lead a horse around. Wearing the halter, the horse learns to walk beside the trainer and to stop when the trainer stops. Once the horse is old enough, it learns to let the trainer put a saddle on it. This action is called saddling up.

The trainer's goal is to saddle up the horse and then get it to bear weight on its back. This may sound like a simple **procedure**, but it's not. It's a long process.

First, the trainer needs to **expose** the horse to all of the things involved in saddling up. The trainer starts off with a saddle pad, which goes on top of the horse, under the saddle. First, the trainer lets the horse smell the saddle pad. Then, the trainer rubs the pad on the horse's belly, legs, and back. When the horse lets the trainer do this, it gets a pat or a scratch as a reward.

The next step is to put the saddle pad on the horse's back, then take it off. Put it on. Take it off. The trainer repeats this process over and over again. It's important to continue an action until the horse gets used to it. It's also important to reward the horse whenever it learns a new part of its training.

When a horse doesn't mind having the saddle pad put on its back, the trainer begins training the horse to wear a saddle. He or she puts the saddle on and takes it off, over and over, until the horse doesn't mind the process. As you can see, **altering** a horse's behavior takes a long time. Horses don't do anything until they decide they are good and ready.

Clydesdales

Is training a horse to pull a load very different from training it to wear a saddle? Let's look at how the Clydesdale, one kind of workhorse, is trained.

Clydesdales are big, reddish-brown, heavyset horses with white, fluffy hair around their feet. They pull the heaviest loads of any horse. Horses that pull heavy loads are called draft horses. The word *draft*, also spelled *draught*, is an Old English word that means "pulling."

Clydesdales have been used as draft horses on farms. They are great at pulling a plow back and forth through a field. They have also been used to pull heavy wagons and sleighs. As big as these draft horses are, Clydesdales are also extremely gentle. You could **accurately** call a Clydesdale a "gentle giant."

So how do Clydesdales learn to do so much hard work? The training takes years. For the first six months of a Clydesdale's life, it stays with its mother on a farm. Once a foal is weaned, it plays in the pastures with other foals. During its first year, a Clydesdale is trained much like the way a horse is trained for riding. It learns to wear a halter and to be led.

During its second year, a Clydesdale learns to wear a harness and saddle. By then, the horse weighs about 1,100 pounds. To get it used to the **placement** of the harness and saddle, the Clydesdale is allowed to run in the fields with the harness and saddle on.

After a Clydesdale's third birthday, there are new lessons to learn. Remember, the Clydesdale is a draft horse. So, the next thing it learns to do is to pull an object.

▲ **You can recognize a Clydesdale by its huge feet, which are covered with fluffy hair.**

By now, a Clydesdale weighs more than 1,500 pounds. Just imagine what a horse this size can pull! Now it's time for the horse to practice pulling. For practice, the trainers give the horse a heavy stone called a boat to pull. The trainer stands on the boat and holds the reins. Then, the horse practices leaning forward into its collar. It keeps leaning forward until it can pull the boat.

Next, the gentle giant is ready for its first horseshoes. These are no ordinary horseshoes. The Clydesdale's horseshoes will be four times as heavy and two times as long as those of the average horse. Each horseshoe weighs five pounds!

With its new shoes on, the Clydesdale is ready to haul a wagon. Six Clydesdales are usually hitched to a typical wagon. Have you ever seen Clydesdales in front of a wagon in a parade? Many of these amazing horses travel around the country **participating** in holiday events.

The wagon drivers snap big reins and shout commands such as "Yah!" to get the Clydesdales moving. To stop the horses, drivers pull back on the reins. The commands are fairly simple—and also fairly easy for the horses to learn.

Horse Dancing

There is another kind of horse training, however, that's very hard for horses to learn. It's even harder for trainers to teach. What is it? This type of training is called dressage. In dressage, a trainer and a horse "dance" together.

A dressage rider gives his or her horse several commands in a row. The horse then makes different moves as **accurately** as possible. It almost looks as if the horse is dancing. There are dressage competitions all around the world. Dressage is even a sport in the Olympic Games!

Training a horse to do a lot of different moves takes patience from the trainer *and* the horse. The best horses for dressage must be very intelligent. They must also be alert and ready to follow commands. Like dancers, they also need to be very strong to do their moves.

Dressage trainers use kindness, patience, and understanding with their special horses. They know a positive approach works best. As a trainer works with a horse over the years, the two become a team. Once the two learn to cooperate well together, they enter competitions.

Dressage teams compete at different levels of difficulty. A dressage team graduates from level to level as the horse learns more and more moves. A dressage team is only allowed to learn more moves after it passes a test on the ones it has already learned. This process of learning more and more moves makes the top dressage horses some of the most educated animals in the world.

Chapter 4

ANIMALS OVERSEAS

Dogs and horses are very popular animals in the United States. In some parts of the world, however, elephants and camels are the most popular animals. Both of these animals are **effective** work animals. They are both very smart and very strong.

As you would expect, elephants are even stronger than Clydesdales. Elephants are used as work animals in several countries in Southeast Asia. These countries include Thailand, Myanmar (Burma), and India. The tradition of using work elephants in these countries goes back thousands of years. Over the years, people have tried many ways to catch these huge animals. Their methods have sometimes been cruel and often have had deadly consequences.

Thousands of years ago in India, people in rural areas dug huge, hidden pits in the ground. An elephant would step on a pit's covering of leaves and sticks and fall in. The trappers then used ropes to raise the animal from the pit. Elephants could be hurt or even die in their fall, and other unwanted animals were often caught in the pits, too. Another, more **effective** method for trapping elephants was practiced for thousands of years in Ceylon, an island near the southeastern coast of the Indian subcontinent. People chased whole herds of elephants into pens. This method, too, was cruel to elephants. Many died.

Why would people trap elephants using such harmful methods? The trappers had little choice. The kings and warriors of the early kingdoms in Southeast Asia demanded a supply of elephants. The gray giants were used to help build palaces and temples. They were sent to war. They also pulled plows on farms, transported goods and people, and helped clear forests.

▲ **These elephants are showing off their log-carrying skills.**

Today, training centers in Southeast Asia breed and train elephants. In Thailand, for instance, elephants are born, raised, and trained at the Young Elephant Training Center. They are taken from their mothers when they are three years old. Where do they go? Straight to elephant school!

People who train Southeast Asian elephants are called mahouts. At the Young Elephant Training Center, the mahouts work closely with the young elephants for seven years.

What do elephants have to learn? They need to be able to follow verbal commands. For instance, elephants that are being trained to work in a forest might have to understand a command to pick up a log. Elephants also must learn to carry a rider and to understand the rider's body signals. Mahouts can direct where they want elephants to go by applying pressure with their feet and legs.

One of a mahout's jobs is to work with an elephant's legs. An elephant must learn to wear chains on its legs so it can be tied to one place. An elephant has more "leg work" to do besides getting used to wearing chains. To help the mahout get up on its back, an elephant needs to learn to raise a front leg and lower its head. The mahout will step on the leg and then climb over the elephant's head in order to ride. The mahout pokes an elephant's legs with sticks to teach it the right movements.

Next, the elephant learns to use its trunk as a tool. For an elephant, its trunk is like a hand. The trunk can grip things and hold and lift them. The mahout uses sugar cane, a sweet snack for elephants, to teach the animal to pick up objects with its trunk. First, the elephant is allowed to eat a few pieces of sugar cane. Then, the seated mahout throws a piece of sugar cane attached to a cord near the elephant. When the elephant picks up the sugar cane to eat it, the mahout pulls the cord attached to the cane, causing the elephant to lift up its trunk. Over time, an elephant learns that when it picks something up with its trunk, it should offer the object to the mahout.

Elephants require a lot of training, but the hard work is worth it. Their working careers can last for decades. Elephants help thousands of people in Southeast Asia to do their jobs. For example, elephants in Thailand haul tons of logs. They can pull two tons of timber more than half a mile without stopping.

It takes several years for an elephant to get used to working with a mahout. Over time, a strong bond forms. In fact, an elephant that has lost its mahout will sometimes refuse to eat. It might even die. The saying that elephants "never forget" is true when it comes to an elephant and its mahout.

Camel Riders

Camels are used in other countries the same way horses are in the United States. Does this seem strange to you? In the United States, we are not used to the idea of riding camels. Think about it. Have you ever seen a movie with ranch hands on camels? Have you seen mounted police officers on camels? Have you even ever seen people training to ride camels at a stable? Probably not. Yet in other parts of the world—such as the deserts of Africa and the Middle East—the sight of a camel rider isn't unusual at all.

There are many reasons why a camel is a good work animal in other parts of the world. A camel can cope with the rough life of a desert. It can stand **exposure** to blazing heat, temperatures that drop quickly at night, and blasts of sand whipped up by winds. It can also live with no food or water for days in a row.

A camel is a calm animal, but it can be stubborn. Camels also often grumble when they are **provoked**, or made to work. However, even though a camel may grumble, it *does* work hard. When treated well, a camel will walk long distances. That's why a camel is sometimes called the "ship of the desert." It can travel a long way.

Also like sailing ships, camels move slowly. To get a camel to move quickly, its rider must prod the camel by tapping it on the neck. Unfortunately for the rider, this method doesn't always work. Usually, camels move at their own pace.

Training a camel is something like training a horse. However, Dr. Charmian Wright, who trains camels, says that there is something camels respond to better than horses do: food!

Dr. Wright is a veterinarian in Utah, as well as an expert camel trainer. You may be wondering why a camel trainer can be found in the United States, when most camels used for work are found in Africa and the Middle East. Actually, there are some camels living in the United States, too. Dr. Wright takes groups of people on camel rides in the Utah desert. She has trained all of her camels herself. They are so well trained, they have even been in the movies!

Because camels are so stubborn, Dr. Wright starts out slowly when she trains them. She uses the following **procedure**. First, she holds out a pan of grain and lets the camel eat. Meanwhile, she pets the camel's neck and head to **convey** that the camel can trust her. Just getting the camel to let her touch it while it is eating may take Dr. Wright weeks of daily or twice-daily lessons.

The next step is to slip a rope over the camel's head while it eats. If the camel pulls away, that's okay. It will come back when it wants more food. Next, Dr. Wright has the camel put its head through a halter before it gets to the grain. Finally, she fastens a halter with a rope.

Just think, the camel and trainer have gone through all this practice, and the camel hasn't even *moved* yet. To get the camel moving, Dr. Wright will tug on the rope. If the camel doesn't move, the trainer pulls harder. As soon as the camel makes a move, Dr. Wright releases the rope. This release eases the pressure on the camel's neck.

Gently and calmly, so as not to **provoke** a camel, a trainer can teach the camel to turn its head, shift its weight, move one leg, move both front legs, and do a full turn. Slowly, the trainer is **conveying** to the camel that the trainer is the "boss camel." Camel herds follow a boss camel. Over time, the trainer becomes a herd's boss camel.

Dr. Wright has a camel named Sefa. This camel has become the boss camel of Dr. Wright's small herd. So, when Dr. Wright is not around, Sefa rules! Sefa is the offspring of another camel in Dr. Wright's herd named Rahji. Rahji came from Australia, where more than 100,000 camels roam free.

There are no wild camels in the United States, but there are several camel farms across the country. At these farms, camels are raised to be ridden at parks and zoos. Some people also use camels for work on farms. These people need to have a lot of patience. Camels really are great service animals—if you have the time to work with them!

▲ **Why are camels sometimes called "ships of the desert"?**

Chapter 5

UNDERWATER INTELLIGENCE

You may have watched dolphins and killer whales **demonstrate** tricks on TV. You may also have seen them perform at an aquarium or a theme park such as SeaWorld®. Chances are, if you watched marine mammals perform in person, you had to decide how close to the tank to sit! It's easy to get soaked when one of these animals slaps its tail on the water or leaps in midair—especially the massive killer whales.

Killer whales have been trained in captivity for only about 25 years. Twenty-five years might seem like a long time to you. But by comparison, people first tamed wild horses about 4,000 years ago. Now *that's* a long time!

Killer whales live in every ocean on Earth. There are two kinds of killer whales. One kind is called residents. The other kind is called transients. Residents stay in one area of the ocean. Transients go wherever they want. Like all species of whales, killer whales live in groups called pods. Pods of residents eat mainly fish. Pods of transients eat mainly mammals such as seals, sea lions, and dolphins.

Why train a killer whale, anyway? By working with killer whales, trainers get a better understanding of their habits, behavior, and level of intelligence. They find out more about how killer whales dive, get along with others, and use their senses. Trainers don't just teach the whales to perform tricks. Whales are also taught behaviors that help their trainers keep an eye on the animals' good health.

There are several SeaWorld theme parks around the country. Each of them has a killer whale that can **demonstrate** complicated routines for theme park visitors. At each SeaWorld, this killer whale is given the name of Shamu®.

None of Shamu's routines resemble the behavior of killer whales in the ocean. So how do the trainers get these huge, mammal-eating predators to do such difficult tricks?

The trainers use positive **reinforcement** every step of the way. Killer whales are rewarded over and over again for taking tiny steps toward a larger goal. First, a trainer looks for a movement that is something like a desired behavior. A whale's good performance is **reinforced** when it makes this movement. The reward is usually food. Other **reinforcers** are a pat, a cool spray of water, or a toy.

It is important that a trainer **reinforce** a desired behavior right away. If a treat comes too late, the whale might think that it is being rewarded for a different behavior than the one desired. So, the trainer uses a "bridge" signal to tell the whale that it has performed correctly. For training whales and dolphins, this bridge signal is usually a whistle. When the animal hears the whistle, it knows it will get a treat.

▶ **A killer whale performs at SeaWorld.**

Why do trainers use whistles? Sounds travel well in water. In fact, whistles are one of the sounds that killer whales make to communicate with each other. So, a whistle makes a good bridge signal to **reinforce** a whale's good behavior.

What is the next step in training a killer whale to perform a new behavior? The trainer teaches the animal to follow, then touch a target. The target is a long stick that has a float on one end. The whale gets its whistle signal and a **reinforcer**, or reward, when it touches the target. Next, the trainer moves the target a bit farther away. Once again, the animal's performance is **reinforced** for touching the target.

Over time, the whale learns to follow the target wherever it is moved. Now, the trainer can use the target to lead the whale through its steps. Eventually, the trainer can **alter** the whale's behavior.

Here's an interesting **aspect** of the training done at SeaWorld. The trainers use underwater tones to help train killer whales. The tones sound like noises made by killer whales in the wild, but a computer produces them. Different tones may stand for a whale's name or an object that is part of a performance. At first, a trainer uses hand signals to direct a whale, while also playing the tone through underwater speakers. After a while, the trainer does not need to use the hand signals. The whale knows to follow the tones.

What if the trainer asks for a certain behavior, and the whale does not respond? Or, what if the whale responds with a different behavior? If this happens, the trainer stays without moving or speaking for several seconds. The whale is never punished. Instead, the behavior simply is not **reinforced**. When the whale finally does that perfect trick in front of an audience, all the trainer's patience and hard work is worth it.

ANIMAL STARS

Shamu isn't the only famous killer whale. A killer whale named Keiko starred in a big Hollywood movie called *Free Willy*. It was the first time a killer whale had been the star of a movie. Of course, it wasn't the first time an animal had been a movie star. Monkeys, cats, and even horses have all made it to the big screen. However, when it comes to the entertainment business, dogs definitely rule.

Dogs have appeared in movies and TV shows since the early days of film and television. Dogs in movies and on TV are called stunt dogs. The tricks they learn to do in front of a camera are called stunts.

Why aren't there more stunt cats and other stunt animals? There are several **factors** to consider. First, cats aren't very good at **interpreting** commands. On the other hand, dogs are very good at learning new tricks. They can learn how to perform a stunt on TV, just as they can learn to help a person cross the street. Dogs also love to please their trainers. This makes them try extra hard to learn the extra hard tricks.

Still, not any dog can become a TV or movie star. First, a dog has to have a good personality. Some dogs are shy, just as some people are shy. There's nothing wrong with being shy—it just doesn't play very well onscreen.

Outgoing, happy dogs have the best chance of becoming a star. A good stunt dog must also enjoy working with people. Another important **factor** to consider is whether or not the dog is comfortable in front of a camera. As you can see, not just any dog will do.

The best stunt dogs also enjoy learning new tricks. For this to happen, a stunt dog and its trainer have to form a strong bond. Before a dog is willing to try certain things, it must trust its trainer. The dog will spend a lot of time practicing before it can become a star.

A dog does a lot of things naturally. Running, barking, and scratching are a few natural dog behaviors. A dog can be taught to do any of these behaviors on command. Yet not all tricks that a stunt dog learns come naturally. For example, a dog can be taught to limp as if its leg is hurt or to put its paws over its eyes. It can take months of training before a dog can correctly **interpret** the commands for these behaviors.

Who is the most famous dog star of all time? That has to be Lassie. The story of Lassie began with a children's story, *Lassie Come Home*, that was published in 1938. Set in England and Scotland, *Lassie* is about a brave female collie. When she is sold to an uncaring master, Lassie escapes and travels more than a thousand miles to return home.

A movie based on *Lassie Come Home* appeared in 1943. Lassie was played by a male dog named Pal. Pal obeyed his trainer's signals very **accurately**. At one point, he dragged himself out of a river. Then, he fell to the ground as if he was tired out from a long and difficult swim. The scene was so moving that the director said, "Pal may have gone into the water, but it was Lassie that came out!"

Oddly, Pal didn't start life as a dog actor. In 1940, Pal was brought to a dog school owned by an animal trainer named Rudd Weatherwax. Pal chased cars and barked a lot. Weatherwax worked with Pal to make him behave better. When it was time for Pal to go back to his owner, the owner said he no longer wanted the dog. Weatherwax was happy to keep Pal. He knew the dog could be a great actor, and he was right.

Where do most trainers find dog superstars? Unlike guide dogs for blind people, which are bred at guide-dog schools, stunt dogs aren't bred anywhere specifically. About 80 percent of stunt dogs are found in animal shelters. In fact, Hollywood trainers often seek out unwanted stray dogs at shelters.

A dog star named Lucky was found at a shelter. His trainer adopted him and began to train him. Lucky went through his training and consequently gained his first role in the film, *Dr. Dolittle*. The actor Eddie Murphy was his human co-star.

Lucky isn't the only dog actor that was saved from a shelter. Fang, a type of dog called a Neapolitan mastiff, went from shelter to stardom after his **placement** in the movie *Harry Potter and the Sorcerer's Stone*. A Jack Russell terrier named Moose was another lucky pup. Moose landed a job as "Eddie" on the TV show *Frasier*. Moose's son, Enzo, is a dog actor, too. Sometimes Enzo played Moose's part on *Frasier*.

▲ **Actor Eddie Murphy with some canine co-stars**

Tricks of the Trade

Dog actors lead pretty good lives. When it's time for their trainers to go to work in the morning, the dogs get to go with them. That means these dogs receive more attention then most pet dogs. Of course, the dogs must work right along with their trainers.

For instance, a dog made it big in New York City by acting in the Broadway musical *Annie*. The dog's trainer, Bill Berloni, taught it all the tricks it would need to know to play its entire part in the play.

Here's how "Sandy," the character played by the dog, learned one of his best tricks. Bill Berloni needed to teach the dog how to crawl. The trick was part of a scene in which Annie first meets the stray dog, Sandy. When Annie calls to him, Sandy comes slowly crawling toward her.

First, the trainer worked on the dog's **placement,** getting it to lie down. Next, Berloni laid down on top of the dog, gently. Holding on to its front legs, Bill moved them back and forth. At the same time, he said, "Crawl." The two practiced over and over. Finally, the dog was on his own. When Bill called out the command, "crawl," the dog knew just what to do. He started to crawl.

Bill Berloni has trained other dogs to perform in musicals. Another dog he trained played the part of Asta in a musical called *Nick and Nora*. Asta was a wire-haired terrier. Berloni had to teach the dog playing Asta to do tricks such as barking every time a telephone rang! This stunt would be pretty tricky for a beginning trainer to teach a dog. However, there are easier tricks you could try out on your favorite dog. For example, you could teach a dog to shake hands, jump, or even kiss.

What is the **procedure** for teaching your dog to give you a kiss? First, make sure you have a gentle dog that you trust before you even try this trick. Then, cover your lips and face with something sticky. Honey works. So does syrup or peanut butter.

Now get down so you are face to face with your dog. Give the command, "wash my face" or, "kiss." Be prepared to get a clean face! When the dog licks the sticky stuff off, give the dog a word of praise and pat it on the back. Do this four or five times. Now try it without the peanut butter. Did the dog lick your face, even without the sticky stuff on it? Over time, the dog should learn to "kiss" your face when it hears the command.

There are some other, general tips that trainers give for training a dog. The most **effective** time to train a dog is before it has been fed. Dogs can get a little sleepy after they eat. Consequently, they will not be as alert and ready to learn right after eating. Also, the treats a trainer gives a stunt dog are not part of a dog's meal. They are used for only training. Dogs love to get a bit of liver or chicken, or a dog biscuit.

When trainers are done working with a dog, they let it know. They do this by using a release word. Some trainers use *Okay* as a dog's release word. Because stunt dogs are asked to stay in one place for a long time, they need to learn this type of command. When the stunt dog hears *Okay*, it knows that it's time to take a break.

Training a stunt dog—or your dog—can be a lot of work. But this work isn't like taking out the garbage or mowing the grass. It's actually a lot of fun.

Given a choice, which of the animals in this book would you choose to train? Would you want to work near water all day? Then, maybe training killer whales and dolphins is for you.

Another **factor** in making this decision is the animals themselves. What type of animal do you like to be around? If you say elephants or camels, you're probably going to have to work at a zoo. Not many people have elephants in their backyard.

However, you may be crazy about horses or dogs. If you have a dog already, you can start training it right now. You may even have a horse. If not, maybe you live near a farm or near stables where there are people who are good at working with horses. Horses are everywhere—even in large cities. If you sign up for lessons or to volunteer at a stable, you should be able to learn a thing or two about training horses.

Getting to know an animal is a lot like getting to know a person. You find out its likes and dislikes. You learn to **comprehend** its personality, whether it is shy or outgoing. If you train your animal right, you also get to know a good friend.

▲ **These Spanish thoroughbreds were trained by a horse breeder in Tijuana, Mexico.**

GLOSSARY

access a way to approach, enter, exit, or make use of

accurately done in a correct way, without mistakes or errors

adapted made to fit for a new use or situation by changing. **Adapting** is changing to fit new conditions.

alter to make something different without completely changing it into something else

ample enough to meet a need or purpose

aspects different ways to think about, or look at, something

astounding filling with wonder or amazement. To **astound** is to fill with wonder or awe.

basically in simplest form; most simply expressed

comprehend to understand the meaning of something

convey to make known

demonstrate to show clearly

deprived taken away from. **Depriving** means not allowing something to be enjoyed.

ecosystem a community of organisms and its environment functioning as a unit

effective successful in making a desired goal happen

endurance the ability to last through a difficult situation; the ability to do something for a long time

evident something that is easily seen or something that is understood, or obvious. **Evidence** is a sign of something, or something that is helpful in forming a conclusion.

exposed showed publicly, or made known

factor a cause or event that makes something happen

indicate to point out. **Indications** are clues or signs about something.

inhabit to live in

interpret to explain or tell the meaning of something

menace a danger or threat. **Menacing** means posing a danger or threat.

migrating moving from one country or region to another. **Migration** means the act of moving from one country or region to another.

nourishment food

participating taking part in

placement the act of putting something in a particular place

procedure a particular way of doing something

provoked annoyed or angered

reinforcement a treat or praise that encourages good behavior. To **reinforce** means to make stronger by adding something.

relatively considered in comparison with something else

substantial a great amount; of great importance; to a large extent

tend to be likely to do or be something; to commonly do or be something

thrive to do very well; to grow a lot

INDEX